SLAVE INSURRECTIONS

AN ACCOUNT

OF

SOME OF THE PRINCIPAL

SLAVE INSURRECTIONS

And others, which have occurred, or been attempted,

in the United States and elsewhere, during

the last two centuries.

With Various Remarks.

Collected from various sources

by

Joshua Coffin

ISBN-13:
978-1535572866

ISBN-10:
1535572868

TO THE READER

The subsequent collection of facts is presented to your notice, with the hope that they will have that effect which facts always have on every candid and ingenuous mind. They exhibit clearly the dangers to which slaveholders are always liable, as well as the safety of immediate emancipation. They furnish, in both cases, a rule which admits of no exception, as it is always dangerous to do wrong, and safe to do right. Please to examine carefully the *whole* account of the revolution in St. Domingo, beginning in March, 1790, and ending in 1802. That exhibits a different picture from that presented in a speech made at the Union-saving meeting lately held in Boston. A part of the truth may be so told as to have all the effect of a deliberate lie.

SLAVE INSURRECTIONS

And they said one to another, We are verily guilty concerning our brother, in that we saw the anguish of his soul when he besought us, and we would not hear; therefore is this distress come upon us.—Gen. 42:21.

Thus said the Lord my God, Feed the flock of the slaughter, whose pastors slay them, and hold themselves not guilty; and they that sell them say, Blessed be the Lord, for I am rich; and their own shepherds pity them not.—Zech. 11:4, 5.

> He that stealeth a man, and *selleth him, or if he be found in his hand,* he shall surely be put to death.—Ex. 21:16.

The late invasion of Virginia by Capt. John Brown and his company has, with all its concomitant circumstances, excited more attention and aroused a more thorough spirit of inquiry on the subject of slavery, than was ever before known. As this is pre-eminently a moral question, and as there is no neutral ground in morals, all intelligent men must ultimately take sides. Every such man must either cherish and defend slavery, or oppose and condemn it, and his vote, if he is an honest man, must accord with his belief. On a question of so momentous importance, "Silence is crime." It demands and will have a thorough investigation, and all attempts to stifle discussion will only accelerate the triumph of the cause they were designed to crush. Thus the denunciation in Congress of Mr. Helper's book, which is in substance only an abstract of facts taken from the last census of the United States, has operated as an extensive advertisement, and will be the means of circulating thousands of copies, where, without such denunciation, it would never have been known. There is in the North, as well as the South, a class of men who act, apparently, on the supposition that those who foresee and foretell any calamity are as guilty as those who create it, and that the only way to obviate any impending danger is not to see it. Such persons not only refuse to see and hear themselves, but do what they can to keep their neighbors in like ignorance.

It has been truly said that "the power of slavery lies in the ignorance, the degradation, the servility of the slaves, and of the non-slaveholding whites

4

of the South, and of the corresponding classes in the Free States. It is through this ignorance and servility that the slaveholders manage to dictate to ecclesiastical bodies, to have power to control pulpits, presses, Colleges, Theological Seminaries, and Missionary and Tract Societies." To keep the blacks and non-slaveholding whites in ignorance is, doubtless, the reason why such pains are taken in Congress to prevent the circulation of Helper's book at the South, which was compiled by a non-slaveholder for the special benefit of the men of his class. The population of the Free States is now about eighteen millions; of the Slave States, eight millions. The slaves number about four millions, who are held as property by only 347,545 persons, men, women and children. This number, small as it is, constituting about one sixth part of the United States, have thus far controlled the legislation of the country. How this power has been acquired is easily understood when we examine the false ideas respecting slavery which are everywhere prevalent; such as the weakness of the public conscience, in the absence of a practical and experimental knowledge of the truth of God's word—in the atheistic notion, prevailing even in the Church and in the ministry, that the unrighteous enactments of wicked me are paramount in authority to the commandments of the Great Jehovah. Hundreds of clergymen, in all parts of the Union, profess to believe that the Bible sanctions American slavery,—a system which, of necessity, cannot exist without a continual violation of every commandment of the Decalogue.

If the Bible sanctions slavery, (as many profess to believe,) why does not the God of the Bible sanction it? In other words, if slavery is sanctioned by the revealed will of God, why are not the dispensations of his providence in accordance with that will? Could it be fairly proved that slavery is in accordance with the will of God, it must necessarily follow that obedience to his will is not only highly advantageous, but perfectly safe; for, surely, no Christian can, for a moment, believe that the providence of God ever militates against the precepts of his word. As, however, the consequences of slavery have been, in all cases, when not averted by timely repentance, disastrous in the extreme, it is therefore undeniably evident that slavery is in direct opposition to the revealed will of God, and, consequently, that those who so violently oppose the abolition of slavery, for fear of supposed dangerous consequences, may truly be said "to know not what they do." The truth on this subject is so plain, and the facts so abundant, that he who runs may read, and know to a certainty the entire safety of immediate emancipation; and that danger arises from liberty withheld, and not from liberty granted. The general opinion seems to be, that the moment you proclaim "liberty to the captive," and make the slave a freeman, be the conditions and restrictions what they may, that moment you make him a vagabond, a thief, and a murderer, whom nothing will satisfy but the blood of those who had been so "fanatical and insane" as to treat him like a human being. Whence this opinion is derived, no one can tell; for it is in direct opposition to reason, common sense, the nature of the human mind, and is entirely unsustained by facts. Indeed, so far as the evidence of facts is concerned, the advocates of immediate abolition have a complete monopoly. All experience proves two things, viz., the entire safety of immediate emancipation, and that all danger has arisen from its indefinite postponement; for this is really the true definition of gradual emancipation.

We all know the results of slavery in Greece and Rome. Troy perished by her slaves in a single night; and as like causes always produce like effects, our obligations to our slaveholding brethren imperiously demand that we should urge on them, in the most earnest manner, the duty of immediately abolishing slavery as their only hope of safety,—the only means by which they can escape the just judgments of God. The safety of immediate emancipation has been proved by Buenos Ayres in 1816, Colombia in 1821, Guatemala in 1824, Peru and Chili in 1828, Mexico in 1829, and especially on the 1st of August, 1834, when 800,000 slaves were set free in a single day in the British West India Islands; and thus far, not a single life has been lost, not a drop of blood shed, in consequence of that beneficent and righteous act. The consequences of holding slaves in bondage, and refusing to emancipate them, have always been disastrous. In our present exemption from slavery in the Free States, we have no cause of boasting, but rather of deep humiliation. We are all involved in the guilt, and must share in the punishment, unless timely and thorough repentance avert the impending blow. To do this effectually, information must be spread, the spirit of inquiry aroused, the temple of God be purified, and "the book of law be read in the ears of all the people," that thus the gross mistakes and misapprehensions which everywhere exist on the subject of slavery and its abolition may be corrected.

Of these mistakes, no one is more prevalent or more dangerous than the one just mentioned, that insurrection, rapine and bloodshed are the necessary consequences of immediate emancipation; and that the only way to avert the evils and the curse of slavery, is to continue in the sin for the present, promise future repentance, and in the meantime, whilst we are preparing to get ready to begin to repent, do every thing that in us lies to extinguish every good feeling, and cultivate and bring into action every bad feeling of the human heart. That such is the belief, and consequent practice, to an alarming extent, throughout our country, and that such a course is impolitic, because it is wicked and dangerous, because it is unjust, facts abundantly show.

Since the abolition of slavery in the British dominions, no trouble has arisen, no danger been feared or apprehended. A thousand John Browns, each with nineteen white men and five black men, could not cause any tumult in any part of the British West Indies. Why is it, then, that one John Brown and company have created so wide-spread an alarm and consternation throughout the Slave States? The Governor of South Carolina has sent a dispatch (Nov. 21) to Gov. Wise, tendering any amount of *military aid to the defence of Virginia!* Gov. Wise had several companies of the military present on the day of the execution of John Brown and others, and assured the Governor of South Carolina that Virginia is able to defend herself. What causes all this tumult and apprehension? SLAVERY! And yet, strange as it may seem, the Virginians, with a stupidity and infatuation which no language can describe, are seriously discussing the propriety of enslaving the free negroes of that State. Such a proceeding would resemble a physician who should order a dose of arsenic to cure a patient who had taken strychnine, or attempt to extinguish a conflagration by throwing oil on the flames.

How the consequences of abolishing slavery would be dreadful and horrible, neither history nor experience informs us. Let us, then, see what they tell us of the consequences of holding men in bondage. In every instance which has fallen under my notice, insurrections have always been projected and carried on by slaves, and never (with the exception of Denmark Vesey in 1822, in Charleston, S. C.) by the free blacks.

The contest between truth and falsehood, right and wrong, justice and injustice, has always continued from the earliest ages to the present moment. More especially is it true concerning American slavery, that "sum of all villanies," a crime which involves the continual violation of every one of the Ten Commandments. I propose, therefore, to give, with other incidents, an abstract of some of the attempts of the oppressed to throw off the yoke which held them, or threatened to hold them, in bondage.

The first instance which has come to my knowledge in this country of an insurrection on a small scale, occurred on Noddle's Island, now East Boston, in 1638. In John Josselyn's account of his first voyage to New England may be found the following. Having previously stated that he was a guest of "Mr. Samuel Maverick, the only hospitable man (as he says) in all the country, giving entertainment to all comers gratis," he thus writes:—

"The second of October about 9 of the clock in the morning Mr. Maverick's negro came to my chamber window, and in her own Countrey language and tune sung very loud and shrill. Going out to her she used a great deal of respect towards me, and willingly would have expressed her grief in English, but I apprehended it by her countenance and deportment, whereupon I repaired to my host to learn of him the cause, and resolved to intreat him on her behalf for that I understood before that she had been a Queen in her own Countrey, and observed a very dutiful garb used toward her by another Negro who was her main. Mr. Maverick was desirous to have a breed of Negroes, and therefore seeing she would not yield by persuasion to company with a Negro young man he had in his house, he commanded him, will'd she, nill'd she, to go to bed with her, but she kickt him out again. This she took in high disdain beyond her slavery, and this was the cause of her grief."

From this statement it appears that Maverick had at least thee slaves: but the number held in the Province, no record informs us. In 1641, the Massachusetts Colony passed the following law:—

"There shall never be any bond slaverie, villinage or captivitie amongst us unless it be lawfull captives taken in just warres, and such strangers as *willingly sell themselves.* And these shall have all the liberties and christian usuages, which the law of God established in Isreal concerning such persons doth morally require. This exempts none from *servitude,* who shall be judged thereto by authority."

"He that stealeth a man, and selleth him, or if *he be found in his hand,* he shall surely be put to death."—Ex. 21:16.

In 1646, one James Smith, a member of Boston church, brought home two negroes from the Coast of Guinea, and had been the means of killing near a hundred more. In consequence of this conduct, the General Court passed the following order:—

"The General Court conceiving themselves bound by the first opportunity to bear witness against the heinous and crying sin of man- stealing, as also to prescribe such timely redress for what is past and such a law for the future, as may sufficiently deter all others belonging to us to have to do in such vile and odious courses, justly abhorred of all good and just men, do order that the negro interpreter with others unlawfully taken, be by the first opportunity at the charge of the country for the present, sent to his native country (Guinea) and a letter with him of the indignation of the Court thereabouts, and justice thereof desiring our honored Governor would please put this order in execution."

From this time till about 1700, the number of slaves imported into Massachusetts was not large. In 1680, Governor Simon Bradstreet, in answer to inquiries from "the lords of his Majesties privy council," thus writes:—

"There had been no company of blacks or slaves brought into the country since the beginning of this plantation, for the space of 50 years, only one small vessell about two yeares since after 20 month's voyage to Madagasca brought hither betwixt 40 and 50 negros, most women and children, sold for 10 pounds, 15 pounds and 20 pounds apiece, which stood the merchants in near 40 pounds apiece one with another: now and then two or three negros are brought hither from Barbados and other of his majesties plantations, and sold her for about 20 pounds apiece, so that there may bee within our government about 100 or 120, and it may bee as many Scots brought hither and sold for servants in the time of the war with Scotland, and most now married and living here, and about halfe so many Irish brought hither at several times as servants."

The number of slaves at this period in the middle and southern colonies is not easily ascertained, as few books, and no newspapers, were published in North America prior to 1704. In that year, the *Weekly News Letter* was commenced, and in the same year the "Society for the propagation of the Gospel in foreign parts opened a catechising school for the slaves at New York, in which city there were then computed to be about 1500 negro and Indian slaves," a sufficient number to furnish materials for the *"irrepressible conflict,"* which had long before begun. The catechist, whom the Society employed, was "Mr. Elias Neau, by nation a Frenchman, who, having made a confession of the Protestant religion in France, for which he had been confined several years in prison, and seven years in the gallies." Mr. Neau entered upon his office "with great diligence, and his labors were very successful; but the negroes were much discouraged from embracing the Christian religion upon account of the very little regard showed them in any religious respect. Their marriages were performed by mutual consent only, without the blessing of the Church; they were buried by those of their own country and complexion, in the common field, without any Christian office; perhaps some ridiculous heathen rites were performed at the grave by some of their own people. No notice was given of their being sick, that they might be visited; on the contrary, frequent discourses were made in conversation, that they had no souls, and perished as the beasts," and "that they grew worse by being taught, and made Christians."

In 1711, May 15, Gov. Gibbes, of South Carolina, in his address to the Legislature of that Province, thus speaks:—

"And, gentlemen, I desire you will consider the great *quantities* of negroes that are daily brought into the government, and the small *number* of whites that comes amongst us: how insolent and mischievous the negroes are become, and to consider the Negro Act already made, doth not reach up to some of the crimes they have lately been guilty of, therefore it might be convenient by some additional clause of said Negro Act to appoint either by gibbets or some such like way, that after executed, they may remain more exemplary than any punishment that hath been inflicted on them."

In the next month, June, the Governor thus writes:—

"We further recommend unto you the repairs of the fortifications about Charleston, and the amending of the Negro Act, *who are of late grown to that height of impudence, that there is scarce a day passes without some robbery or insolence, committed by them in one part or other of this province.*"

"In the year 1712," says the Rev. D. Humphreys, "a considerable number of negroes of the Carmantee and Pappa Nations formed a plot to destroy all the English, *in order to obtain their liberty;* and kept their conspiracy so secret, that there was no suspicion of it till it came to the very execution. However, the plot was by God's Providence happily defeated. The plot was this. The negroes sat fire to a house in York city, and Sunday night in April, about the going down of the moon. The fire alarmed the town, who from all parts ran to it; the conspirators planted themselves in several streets and lanes leading to the fire, and shot or stabbed the people

10

as they were running to it. Some of the wounded escaped, and acquainted the Government, and presently by the firing of a great gun from the fort, the inhabitants were called under arms and pretty easily scattered the negroes; they had killed about 8 and wounded 12 more. In their flight some of them shot themselves, others their wives, and then themselves; some absconded a few days, and then killed themselves for fear of being taken; but a great many were taken, and 18 of them suffered death. This wicked conspiracy was at first apprehended to be general among all the negroes, and opened the mouths of many to speak against giving the negroes instruction. Mr. Neau durst hardly appear abroad for some days; his school was blamed as the main occasion of this barbarous plot. On examination, only two of all his school were so much as charged with the plot, and on full trial the guilty negroes were found to be such as never came to Mr. Neau's school; and what is very observable, the persons, whose negroes were found to be most guilty, were such as were the declared opposers of making them Christians. However a great jealousy was now raised, and the common cry very loud against instructing the negroes."

From the *Boston Weekly Journal,* of April 8th, 1724, I make the following extract:—

"Every reasonable man ought to remember their *first* villanous attempt at New York, and how many good innocent people were murdered by tem, and had it not been for the garrison there, that city would have been reduced to ashes, and the greatest part of the inhabitants murdered."

On the 6th of May, 1720, the negroes of South Carolina murdered Mr. Benjamin Cattle, a white woman, and a negro boy. Forces were immediately raised, and sent after them, twenty-three of whom were taken, six convicted, three executed, and three escaped.

In October, 1722, about two hundred negroes near the mouth of the Rappahannock river, Virginia, got together in a body, armed with an intent to kill the people in church, but were discovered, and fled.

On the 13th of April, 1723, Gov. Dummer issued a proclamation with the following preamble, viz.:—

"Whereas within some short time past, many fires have broke out within the town of Boston, and divers buildings have thereby been consumed:

which fires have been designedly and industriously kindled by some villanous and desperate Negroes, or other dissolute people, as appears by the confession of some of them (who have been examined by authority) and many concurring circumstances; and it being vehemently suspected that they *have entered into a combination to burn and destroy the town,* I have therefore thought fit, with the advice of his Majesty's Council, to issue forth this Proclamation," &c.

On the 18th of April, 1723, Rev. Joseph Sewall preached a discourse, particularly occcasioned "by the late fires yt have broke out in Boston, supposed to be purposely set by ye Negroes." [FN#1]

[FN#1] Diary of Rev. Samuel Dexter.

On the next day, April 19th, the Selectmen of Boston made a report to the town on the subject, consisting of nineteen articles, of which the following is No. 9:—

"That if more than Two Indians, Negro or Molatto Servants or Slaves be found in the Streets or Highways in or about the Town, idling or lurking together unless in the service of their Master or Employer, every one so found shall be punished at the House of Correction."

So great at that time were the alarm and danger in Boston, occasioned by the slaves, that in addition to the common watch, a military force was not only kept up, but at the breaking out of every fire, a part of the militia were ordered out under arms to keep the slaves in order!!

The report of nineteen articles, submitted to the town of Boston, was finally embodied in a Negro Act of fifteen sections, of which the 15th was as follows:—

"That no Indian, negro or mullatto, upon the breaking out of fire and the continuance thereof during the night season, shall depart from his or her master's house, nor be found in the streets at or near the place where the fire is, upon pain of being forthwith seized and sent to the common gaol, and afterwards whipt, three days following before dismist, &c."

From the *N. E. Courant,* Nov. 1724, I take the following extract:—

"It is well known what loss the town of Boston sustained by fire not long since, *when almost every night* for a considerable time together, some building or other and sometimes several in the same night were either burned to the ground or some attempts made to do it. It is likewise well known that those villanies were carried on by Negro servants, the like whereof we never felt before from unruly servants, nor ever heard of the like happening in any place attended with the like circumstances."

Like causes produce like effects. Since the abolition of slavery in Massachusetts, no one has felt alarmed at seeing "two or more colored men lurking together" in Boston. Prior to the abolition of slavery in the British West Indies, the militia were always called out under arms on the Christmas holidays, in order to prevent any attempts at insurrection among the slaves. Since that time, there has been no apprehension of any disturbances, and, of course, no calling out of the militia.

In 1728, an insurrection of slaves occurred in Savannah, Georgia, who were fired on twice before they fled. They had formed a plot to destroy all the whites, and nothing prevented them but a disagreement about the mode. At that time, the population consisted of 3000 whites and 2700 blacks.

In January, 1729, the slaves in Antigua conspired to destroy the English, which was discovered two or three days before the intended assault. Of the three conspirators, *two were burnt alive!!* *"'Twas admirable,"* says the account, *"to see how long they stood before they died, the great wood not readily burning, and their cry was water, water!"*

In August, 1730, an insurrection of blacks occurred in Williamsburgh, Va., occasioned by a report, on Col. Spotswood's arrival, that he had direction from his Majesty to free all baptized persons. The negroes improved this to a great height. Five counties were in arms pursuing them, with orders to kill them if they did not submit.

In August, 1730, the slaves in South Carolina conspired to destroy all the whites. This was the first open rebellion in that State, where the negroes were actually armed and embodied, and took place on the Sabbath.

In the same month, a negro man plundered and burned a house in Malden, (Mass.) and gave this reason for his conduct, that his master had sold him to a man in Salem, whom he did not like.

In 1731, Capt. George Scott, of R. I. was returning from Guinea with a cargo of slaves, who rose upon the ship, murdered three of the crew, all of whom soon after died, except the captain and boy.

In 1732, Capt. John Major, of Portsmouth, N. H., was murdered, with all his crew, and the schooner and cargo seized by the slaves.

In December, 1734, Jamaica was under martial law, and two thousand soldiers ordered out after the "rebellious negroes."

In the same year, an insurrection occurred in Burlington, (Pa.) among the blacks, whom the account styles *"intestine and inhuman enemies, who in some places have been too much indulged."* Their design was as soon as the season was advanced, so that they could lie in the woods, on a certain night, agreed on by some hundreds of them, and kept secret a long time, that every negro and negress should rise at midnight, kill every master and his sons, sparing the women, kill all the draught horses, set all their houses and barns on fire, and secure all their saddle horses for flight towards the Indians in the French interest.

In 1735, the slaves of the ship Dolphin, of London, on the coast of Africa, rose upon the crew; but being overpowered, they got into the powder room, and to be revenged, blew up themselves with the crew.

In 1739, there were three formidable insurrections of the slaves in South Carolina—one in St. Paul's Parish, one in St. Johns, and one in Charleston. In one of these, which occurred in September, they killed in one night twenty-five whites, and burned six houses. They were pursued, attacked, and fourteen killed. In two days, twenty more were killed, and forty were taken, some of whom were shot, some hanged, and some *gibbeted alive!* This "more exemplary" punishment, as Gov. Gibbes called it, failed of its intended effect, for the next year there was another insurrection in South Carolina. There were then above 40,000 slaves, and about twenty persons were killed before it was quelled.

In 1741, there was a formidable insurrection among the slaves in New York. At that time the population consisted of 12,000 whites and 2,000 blacks. Of the conspirators, thirteen were *burned alive,* eighteen hung, and eighty transported.

Those who were transported were sent to the West India Islands. As a specimen of the persons who were suitable for transportation, I give the following from the *Boston Gazette,* Aug. 17, 1761:—

"To be sold, a *parcel* of likely young negroes, imported from Africa, cheap for cash. Inquire of John Avery. Also, if any person have any negro men, strong and hearty, *though not of the best moral character, which are proper subjects for transportation, they may have an exchange for small negroes."*

In 1747, the slaves on board of a Rhode Island ship commanded by Capt. Beers, rose, when off Cape Coast Castle, and murdered the captain and all the crew, except the two mates, who swam ashore.

In 1754, C. Croft, Esq., of Charleston, S. C., had his buildings burned by his female negroes, *two of whom were burned alive!!*

In September, 1755, Mark and Phillis, slaves, were put to death at Cambridge, (Mass.) for poisoning their master, Mr. John Codman of Charlestown. Mark was hanged, and *Phillis burned alive!* Having ascertained that their master had, by his will, made them free at his death, they poisoned him in order to obtain their liberty so much the sooner.

In August, 1759, another insurrection was contemplated in Charleston, S. C.

In October, 1761, there was a rebellion among the slaves in Kingston, Jamaica; and in the next December, the slaves in Bermuda rebelled, and threatened to destroy all the whites. All were engaged in the plot, which was accidentally discovered. *One was burned alive,* one hanged, and eleven condemned.

In the same year, Capt. Nichols, of Boston, lost forty of his slaves by an insurrection, but saved his vessel.

In 1763, the Dutch settlement at Barbetias was surprised and destroyed by the negroes.

In 1764, the slaves in Jamaica projected a rebellion, and intended to destroy all the whites on the island.

In 1767, there was a rebellion among the slaves in Grenada.

In 1768, when Gen. Gage was in command of the British troops in Massachusetts, one Capt. John Wilson, of the 59th regiment, made an attempt to excite the few slaves in Boston (about 300) to rise against their masters. He assured the slaves that the foreign troops had come to procure their freedom, and that "with their assistance, they would be able to drive the Liberty Boys to the devil." In October, the Selectmen made a complaint against him; had him arrested, and bound over for trial, but by the influence of British officials, the indictment was quashed, and Wilson fled, satisfied that Boston would not be a safe place for *him*.

In 1765, symptoms of a rebellious and insurrectionary spirit were manifested in various parts of the thirteen colonies, then nominally at least subjects of King George. This spirit was aroused by the passage, by the British Parliament, of the Stamp Act on the 22d of March of that year. As the British government were unable to enforce this Act, it was graciously repealed on the 22d of February, 1766, but coupled with the declaratory Act, that "the Legislature of Great Britain had authority to bind the colonies in all cases whatsoever." On the 20th of November, 1767, the Act previously passed, imposing a duty of three pence per pound on tea, was to take effect. From this Act, with other causes combined, many commotions were excited anew among the people. On the 5th of March, 1770, the Boston massacre occurred. The skirmish at Lexington and Concord on the 19th of April, and the battle on Breed's hill on the 17th of June, 1775, greatly increased the excitement. About the middle of July, the year Lord Dunmore, the royal governor of Virginia, ceased to exercise the functions of his office, having with his wife and children, for fear of the people, taken refuge on board the Fowey man of war. With the hope that he should succeed in reducing the Virginians to subjection, Lord Dunmore gave out that he should instigate the slaves, who were extremely numerous, to revolt against their masters. The dread of the consequences of such a revolt decided the Virginians to form a convention, in which they placed great confidence. The governor expected, but in vain, that the people would rise, and take arms in favor of the king. Hoping, however, that with such force as he had, and the frigates on that station, he should make some impression on the surrounding country, he surprised the town of Hampton, situated on the bay of the same name, and devoted it to the flames. He then proclaimed martial law, "declared free all slaves or servants, black or white, belonging to rebels, provided they would take up arms and join the royal troops." The governor again came on shore at

Norfolk, where some hundreds of loyalists and negroes joined the governor. With this motley force, aided by two hundred soldiers of the line, he made an unsuccessful attack on the provincials on the 9th of December. He again repaired on board of one of the ships, and on the first of January, 1776, the frigate Liverpool, two corvettes and the governor's armed sloop, opened a terrible fire on the city; and at the same time, a detachment of marines landed, and set fire to the houses. In this manner was destroyed on of the most opulent and flourishing cities of Virginia.

On the 4th of July, 1776, after eleven years of unavailing negotiation and some fighting, the delegates of the thirteen Colonies, not believing the modern dogma that, however bad the laws may be, they must be obeyed till they are repealed, raised the standard of rebellion, and bade defiance to the colossal power of Great Britain, declaring that they were, and of right ought to be, free and independent, and making the following declaration, viz.:—

"We hold these truths to be self-evident: that all men are created equal; that they are endowed by their Creator with certain inalienable rights; that among these are life, liberty, and the pursuit of happiness."

This was an insurrection on a great scale; and as the insurgents were *white* men, and were successful, they were, of course, right. Says Jefferson, in 1814, "What an incomprehensible machine is man! who can endure toil, famine, stripes, imprisonment, and death itself, in vindication of his own liberty; and the next moment be deaf to all those motives, whose power supported him through his trials, and inflict on his fellow-man a bondage, *one hour of which is fraught with more misery than ages of that which he rose in rebellion to oppose.*"

The insurrection of the people of France against their king, which is generally called the French revolution, is with all its horrors too well known to require notice.

The scenes of St. Domingo next claim our attention. The incidents are given in the language of an author, whose name I do not recollect.

When the French Revolution, which decreed equality of rights to all citizens, had taken place, the *free people of color* of St. Domingo, many of whom were persons of large property and liberal education, petitioned the General Assembly that they might enjoy the same political privileges as the whites. At length, in March, 1790, the subject of the petition was discussed, when the Assembly adopted a decree concerning it. The decree, however, was worded so ambiguously, that the two parties in St. Domingo—the *whites* and the *people of color*—interpreted each in their own favor. This difference of interpretation gave rise to animosities between them, which were augmented by political party spirit, according as they were royalists, or partisans of the French revolution, so that disturbances took place, and blood was shed.

In the year 1791, the people of color petitioned the Assembly again, but principally for an explanation of the decree in question.

On the 15th of May, the subject was taken into consideration, and the result was another decree in more explicit terms, which determined that the people of color in all the French islands were entitled to all the rights of citizens, provided they were born of *free parents on both sides.* The news of this decree no sooner arrived at the Cape, than it produce an indignation almost amounting to frenzy among the whites. They directly trampled under foot the national cockade, and with difficulty were prevented from seizing all the merchant ships in the roads. After this, the two parties armed against each other. Even camps began to be formed. Horrible massacres and conflagrations followed, the reports of which, when brought to the mother country, were so terrible that the Assembly rescinded the decree in favor of the people of color in the same year.

In 1792, the news of this new decree reached St. Domingo, and produced as much irritation among the people of color, as the news of the former had done among the whites; and hostilities were renewed on both sides.

As soon as these events became known in France, the Conventional Assembly, which had then succeeded the Legislature, seeing no hope of reconciliation on either side, knew not what other course to take than to do justice, whatever the consequences might be. They resolved accordingly, in the month of April, that the decree of 1791, which had been first made and reversed by the preceding Assembly, should be made good; thus restoring to the people of color the privileges which had been voted to them; and they appointed Santhonax, Polverel, and another to repair as Commissioners to St. Domingo, with a large body of troops, in order to enforce the decree, and to keep the peace.

In the year 1793, the same division and bloodshed continuing, notwithstanding the arrival of the commissioners, a very trivial matter, a quarrel between a mulatto and a white man, (an officer in the French marines,) gave rise to new disasters. The quarrel took place at Cape Francois on the 20th of June. On the same day, the seamen left their ships in the roads, and came on shore, and made common cause with the white inhabitants of the town. On the other side were ranged the mulattoes and other people of color, and these were afterwards joined by some insurgent blacks. The battle lasted nearly two days. During this time, the arsenal was taken and plundered, some thousands were killed in the streets, and more than half of the town was burned. The commissioners, who were witnesses of the horrible scene, and who had done all that they could to restore peace, escaped unhurt; but they were left upon a heap of ruins, and with little more power than the authority which their commission gave them. They had only about a thousand troops left in the place. They determined, therefore, under these circumstances, to call in the slaves in their neighborhood to their assistance. They issued a proclamation in consequence, by which they promised to give *freedom to all the blacks who were willing to range themselves under the banner of the republic.*

This was the first proclamation made by public authority for emancipating slaves in St. Domingo, and was usually called the proclamation of Santhonax. The result of it was, that a considerable number of slaves came in, and were enfranchised.

Soon after this transaction, Polverel left his colleague, Santhonax, at the Cape, and went in his capacity of commissioner to Port au Prince, the capital of the West. Here he found every thing quiet, and cultivation in a flourishing state. From Port au Prince he visited Aux Cayes, the capital of the South. He had not, however, been long there, before he found that the minds of the slaves began to be in an unsettled state. They had become acquainted with what had taken place in the North; not only with the riots at the Cape, but the proclamation of Santhonax. Polverel, therefore, seeing the impression which it had begun to make on the minds of the slaves in these parts, was convinced that emancipation could neither be prevented, nor even retarded; and that it was absolutely necessary, for *the personal safety of the white planters,* that it should be extended to *the whole island.* He was so convinced of the necessity of this, that in September, 1793, *he drew up a proclamation without further delay to that effect,* and put it into circulation. He dated it from Aux Cayes. He exhorted the planters to patronise it. He advised them, if they wished to avoid the most serious calamities, to concur themselves in the proposition of giving freedom to their slaves. He then caused a registry to be opened at the government house, to receive the signatures of those who should approve of his advice. It was remarkable that all the proprietors in these parts inscribed their names in this book. He then caused a similar registry to be opened at Port au Prince for the West. Here the same disposition was found to prevail. All the planters, except one, gave in their signatures. They had become pretty generally convinced, by this time, that their own personal safety was connected with the measure. We may now add that, in the month of February, 1794, the Conventional Assembly of France passed a decree for the abolition of slavery *throughout the whole of the French Colonies.* Thus the government of the mother country confirmed freedom to those, on whom it had been bestowed by the commissioners. This decree, therefore, *put the finishing stroke to the whole.* It completed the emancipation of *the whole slave population of St. Domingo.*

With regard to the conduct of those who were emancipated by Santhonax in the North, I find nothing particular to communicate. With respect to those emancipated in the South and West by Polverel, we are enabled to give a pleasing account. Colonel Malenfant, who was residing in the island at the time, has made us acquainted with their general conduct and character. "After the public act of emancipation," says he, (by Polverel,) "the *negroes remained quiet, both in the South and in the West, and they continued to work on all the plantations.* There were, indeed, estates which had neither owners nor managers resident on them. Some of these had been put in prison by Mount Brun; and others, fearing the same fate, had fled to the quarter which had just been given up to the English. Yet on these estates, though abandoned, *the negroes continued their labors,* where there were any (even inferior) agents to guide them; and on those estates where no white men were left to direct them, they betook themselves to the planting of provisions; but on all the plantations where the *whites resided,* the *blacks continued to labor as quietly as before."*

A little further on, in the same work, ridiculing the notion entertained in France, that the negroes would not work without compulsion, he takes occasion to allude to other negroes who had been liberated by the same proclamation, but who were more immediately under his own eye. "If," says he, "you will take care not to speak to them of their return to slavery, but talk to them about their liberty, you may, with this latter word, chain them down to labor. How did Toussaint succeed? How did I succeed also, before his time, in the plain of the Cul de Sac, and on the plantation

Gouraud, more than eight months after liberty had been granted (by Polverel) to the slaves? Let those who knew me at the time, and even the blacks themselves, be asked. They will all reply that *not a single negro* on that plantation, consisting of more than 460 laborers, *refused to work;* and yet this plantation was thought to be under the worst discipline, and the slaves the most idle in the plain. I, myself, inspired the same activity into three other plantations, of which I had the management."

The above account is far beyond any thing that could have been reasonably expected; indeed, it is most gratifying. We find that the liberated negroes, *both in the South and West,* continued to work on *their old plantations,* and for *their old masters;* so that there was also a spirit of industry among them; for they are described as continuing to work *as quietly as before.* Such was the conduct of the negroes for the first nine months after their liberation, up to the middle of 1794. Of the conduct of the negroes during the year 1795, and part of 1796, I find no account. Had there been any outrages, they would have been mentioned. Let no one connect the outrages, which assuredly took place in St. Domingo in 1791 and 1792, *with the effects of the emancipation of the slaves.* The great massacres and conflagrations which at that time made so frightful a picture in the history of this unhappy island, occurred *in the days of slavery,* before the proclamation of Santhonax and Polverel, and before the great conventional decree of the mother country was known. They had been occasioned, too, *not originally by the slaves themselves,* but by quarrels between the *white* and *colored* planters, and between the *royalists* and the *revolutionists,* who, for the purpose of wreaking their vengeance on each other, called in the aid of their slaves; and as to the insurgent negroes of the North, who filled that part of the colony in those years with terror and dismay, they were originally put in motion, according to Malenfant, *by the royalists themselves,* to strengthen their own cause, and to put down *the partisans of the French revolution.*

When Jean Francois and Brasson commenced the insurrection, there were many white royalists among them, and the negroes were made to wear the white cockade.

I now come to the latter part of the year 1796, and we shall find that there was no want of industry or of obedience in those who had been emancipated. *"The colony,"* says Malenfant, *"was flourishing under Toussaint; the whites lived happily on their estates, and the negroes continued to work for them."* Now, Toussaint came into power, being

21

General-in-chief of the armies of St. Domingo, near the end of the year 1796, and remained in power till the year 1802, or till the invasion of the island by the French expedition by Bonaparte, under Le Clerc. Malenfant, therefore, means to state that from 1796 to 1802, a period of six years, the planters and farmers kept possession of their estates; that they lived on them peacefully, and without interruption or disturbance; and that the negroes, though they had all been set free, continued to be their laborers.

Gen. La Croix, who published his "Memoirs for a History of St. Domingo" at Paris in 1819, informs us that when Santhonax returned to the colony in 1796, *"he was astonished at the state in which he found it on his return."* This, says, La Croix, was owing to Toussaint, who, while he had succeeded in establishing perfect order and discipline among the black troops, had succeeded in making the black laborer return to the plantation, there to resume the drudgery of cultivation.

But the same author tells us that, in the next year, 1797, the most wonderful progress had been made in agriculture. He uses these remarkable words:—*"The colony marched as by enchantment to its former splendor; cultivation prospered; every day produced perceptible proofs of its progress. The city of the Cape and the plantations of the North rose up again visibly to the eye."* To effect this wonderful improvement, many circumstances conspired, but principally the fact that the negroes, being free, had a powerful motive to be industrious and obedient.

The next witness is Gen. Vincent, who was a colonel, and afterwards a general of brigade of artillery at St. Domingo, and was there during the time of Santhonax and Toussaint. He was called to Paris by Toussaint, when he arrived just at the moment of the peace of Amiens, and found, to his inexpressible surprise and grief, that Bonaparte was preparing an immense armament, to be commanded by Le Clerc, for the purpose of *restoring slavery in St. Domingo!* Against this expedition, the General remonstrated with the First Consul, telling him that, though the army destined for this purpose was composed of the brilliant conquerors of Europe, it would do nothing in the Antilles, and would assuredly be destroyed by the climate of St. Domingo, if not destroyed by the blacks. He stated that every thing was going on well in St. Domingo and therefore conjured him, in the name of humanity, not to attempt to reverse this beautiful order of things. His efforts were ineffectual. The armament sailed, and, arriving on the shores of St. Domingo, a scene of blood and torture followed, *such as history had seldom if ever before disclosed,* which, though *planned and executed by whites,* all the barbarities said to have been perpetrated *by the insurgent blacks of the North* amounted comparatively to nothing. At length, the survivors of that vast army were driven from the island, with the loss of sixty thousand lives. Till that time, the planters had retained their estates; and then it was, and not till then, that they lost their all. The question may be asked, why did the First Consul make this frightful invasion? It was owing, not to the emancipated negroes, who were *peaceful, industrious, and beyond example happy,* but to the prejudices of their former masters—prejudices common to almost all slaveholders. Accustomed to the use of arbitrary power, they could not brook the loss of their whips. Accustomed to look down on the negroes as an inferior race of beings, as mere reptiles of the earth, they could not bear, peaceably as these had conducted themselves, to come into that familiar contact with them as free laborers, which the change in their condition required. They considered them, too, as property lost, and which was to be recovered. In an evil hour, they prevailed on Bonaparte, by false representations and *promises of pecuniary support,* to undertake to restore things to their former state; and the result is before the world as an example and a warning. When will our slaveholding brethren learn that the advocates of immediate emancipation are the only true friends of both slaveholders and slaves, and that the only path of safety is the path of duty, which demands the immediate repentance of all sin, and especially that "sum of all villanies," slavery?

In the year 1800, the city of Richmond, Va., and indeed the whole slaveholding country were thrown into a state of intense excitement, consternation and alarm, by the discovery of an intended insurrection among the slaves. The plot was laid by a slave named Gabriel, who was claimed as the property of Mr. Thomas Prosser. A full and true account of this General Gabriel, and of the proceedings consequent on the discovery of the plot, has never yet been published. In 1831 a short account, which is false in almost every particular, appeared in the Albany *Evening Journal* under the head of "Gabriel's Defeat." It was the same year republished in the first volume of the *Liberator,* and during the last year (1859) has been extensively republished in many other papers. The following is the copy of a letter dated Sept. 21, 1800, written by a gentleman of Richmond, Va., and published in the Boston *Gazette,* Oct. 6th:—

"By this time, you have no doubt heard of the conspiracy, formed in this country by the negroes, which, but for the interposition of Providence,

23

would have put the metropolis of the State, and even the State itself, into their possession. A dreadful storm with a deluge of rain, which carried away the bridges and rendered the water courses every where impassable, prevented the execution of their plot. *It was extensive and vast in its design. Nothing could have been better contrived. The conspirators were to have seized on the magazine, the treasury, the mills, and the bridges across James river.* They were to have entered the city of Richmond in three places with fire and sword, to commence an indiscriminate slaughter, the French only excepted. They were then to have called on their fellow negroes and the friends of humanity throughout the continent, by proclamation, to rally round their standard. The magazine, which was defenceless, would have supplied them with arms for many thousand men. The treasury would have given them money, the mills bread, and the bridges would have enabled them to let in their friends, and keep out their enemies. Never was there a more propitious season for the accomplishment of their purpose. The country is covered with rich harvests of Indian corn; flocks and herds are every where fat in the fields; and the liberty and equality doctrine, nonsensical and wicked as it is, (in this land of tyrants and slaves,) is for electioneering purposes sounding and resounding through our valleys and mountains in every direction. The city of Richmond and the circumjacent country are in arms, and have been so for ten or twelve days past. The patrollers are doubled through the State, and the Governor, impressed with the magnitude of the danger, has appointed for himself three Aids de Camp. A number of conspirators have been hung, *and a great many more are yet to be hung.* The trials and executions are going on day by day. Poor deluded wretches! *Their democratic deluders, conscious of their own guilt, and fearful of the public vengeance, are most active in bringing them to punishment. "Quicquid delirant reges, plectuntur Achivi"!* Two important facts have been established by the witnesses on the different trials. First, that the plan of the plot was drawn by two Frenchmen in Richmond, and by them given to the negro General Gabriel, who is not yet caught; and secondly, that in the meditated massacre, *not one Frenchman* was to be touched. It is moreover believed, though not positively known, that a great many of our profligate and abandoned whites (who are distinguished by the burlesque appellation of *democrats*) are implicated with the blacks, and would have joined them if they had commenced their operations. The particulars of this horrid affair you will probably see detailed in Davis' paper from Richmond, but certainly in Stewart's paper in Washington. The Jacobin printers and their friends are panic struck. Never was terror more strongly depicted in the countenances of men. They see, they feel, the fatal mischiefs that their preposterous principles and ferocious party spirit have brought upon us."

The Virginia *Gazette* of Sept. 12th thus writes:—"The public mind has been much involved in dangerous apprehensions concerning an insurrection of the negroes in several of the adjoining counties. Such a thing has been in agitation by an ambitious and insidious fellow named Gabriel, the property of Mr. Thomas Prossor. * * * * Yesterday a Court was held at the Court House in this city, when six of them were convicted, and condemned to be executed this day, Sept. 12th."

"On Thursday, Sept. 18th," says the New York *Spectator,* "five more were executed near the city of Richmond, who were concerned in the insurrection."

These eleven negroes were executed before the apprehension of Gen. Gabriel, for whose arrest Gov. Monroe offered a reward of $300. The following is a copy of a letter dated Norfolk, Sept. 25th, 1800:—

"Last Tuesday, on information being given that Gen. Gabriel was on board the three-masted schooner Mary, Richardson Taylor skipper, just arrived from Richmond, he was committed to prison in irons. It appeared on his examination that he went on board on the 14th inst., four miles below Richmond, and remained on board eleven days; that when he went first on board, he was armed with a bayonet and bludgeon, both of which he threw into the river."

"On Saturday last," (Sept. 27th,) says a Richmond paper, "the noted Gabriel arrived here by water, under guard from Norfolk, and was committed to the Penitentiary for trial. We understand that when he was apprehended, he manifested the greatest marks of firmness and composure, showing not the least disposition to equivocate, or screen himself from justice. He denied the charge of being the first in exciting the insurrection, although he was to have had the chief command, but that there were four or five persons more materially concerned in the conspiracy, and said that he could mention several in Norfolk; but being conscious of meeting with the fate of those before him, he was determined to make no confession."

"It was stated," says a New York paper, "to be the best planned and most matured of any before attempted." "Gabriel was condemned," says another paper, "on the 3d of October, and executed on the 7th, (having been respited from the 4th,) without making any *useful* confession. On the 3d of October, ten more negroes were executed, and on the 7th, fifteen more— viz.: five at the Brook, five at Four Mile Creek, and four with Gabriel at the Richmond gallows."

These fifteen, as far as we have any account, were the last who were either executed or tried. The Court, in their eager haste to apprehend and punish the conspirators, of whom five, six, ten and fifteen at a time were executed, and that only the day after trial, of whom not one had committed any overt act, and against whom no testimony appears to have been furnished by any white witness, found, after the apprehension of General Gabriel, that they had made some sad mistakes. This fact, with others, caused such a revulsion of feeling, and excited so great a sympathy in behalf of the poor creatures, that they were obliged, by a moral necessity, to pause in their course.

Under date of Oct. 13th, the *Commercial Advertiser* thus writes:—

"The trials of the negroes concerned in the late insurrection are suspended until the opinion of the Legislature can be had on the subject. *This measure is said to be owing to the immense numbers, who are implicated in the plot, whose death, should they all be found guilty and be executed, will nearly produce the annihilation of the blacks in this part of the country.*"

The next day, Oct. 14th, a correspondent from Richmond makes a similar statement with this addition:—

"A conditional amnesty is perhaps expected. At the next session of the Legislature of Virginia, they took into consideration the subject referred to them, *in secret session, with closed doors.* The *whole* result of their deliberations has never yet been made public, as the injunction of secrecy has never been removed. To satisfy the Court, the public, and themselves, they had a task so difficult to perform, that it is not surprising that their deliberations were in secret."

From 1800 till 1816, nothing was divulged. In the spring of 1816, the Hon. Charles Fenton Mercer, in a speech delivered by him in 1833, says, "The intelligence broke in upon me, like a ray of light through the profoundest gloom, and by a mere accident, which occurred in the spring of 1816, that, upon two several occasions, the General Assembly of Virginia had invited the United States to obtain a territory beyond their limits, whereon to colonize *certain portions* of our colored population. For the evidence of these facts, *then new to me,* I was referred to the Clerk of the Senate; and in the *private records* I found them verified."

On the 21st of December, 1800, the Virginia House of Delegates passed, in *secret session,* the following resolution:—

"Resolved, That the Governor [Monroe] be requested to correspond with the President of the United States, on the subject of purchasing land without the limits of this State, *whither persons obnoxious to the laws, or dangerous to the peace of society, may be removed."*

The General Assembly of Virginia, having through their agent, Mr. Jefferson, failed in 1800, 1802 and 1804, to obtain a place of *banishment* for that portion of their colored population whom they were afraid to hang, and unwilling to pardon, passed on Jan. 22, 1805, still in *secret session,* the following resolution:—

"Resolved, That the Senators of this State in the Congress of the United States be instructed, and the Representatives be requested, to exert their best efforts for the obtaining from the General Government a competent portion of territory in the country of Louisana, to be appropriated to the residence of *such people of color as have been, or shall be, emancipated, or may hereafter become dangerous to the public safety,"* &c.—[See African Repository, June, 1832, and November, 1833.]

The Legislature of Virginia having failed in all their attempts to find a suitable Botany Bay, to which the free people of color, convicts, and other dangerous persons could be banished, passed in 1805 a law prohibiting emancipation, except on the condition that the emancipated should leave the State; or, if remaining in the State more than twelve months, should be sold by the overseers of the poor for the benefit of the Literary Fund.

Here we see another consequence of the attempt of slaves to obtain their freedom, viz., an increased persecution of the free people of color, a law to prevent their increase, and a desire to banish all of them from the State. The conspiracy of Gen. Gabriel and his coadjutors was, therefore, the occasion, if not the cause, of the formation, in 1817, of the Colonization Society, whose great object was, by removing all disturbing causes, to make slavery secure, lucrative, and perpetual. Another noticeable fact, made manifest by the intended insurrection, is the state of fearful insecurity in which the residents of a slaveholding community must feel that they are living. The late assertion of Gov. Wise, that "We, the Virginians, are in no danger from our slaves or the colored people,"— or that of Senator Mason, "We can take care of ourselves,"—or that of Miles, of South Carolina, "We are impregnable,"—betrays the depth and extent of their fear by the very attempt to conceal it; like timid boys "ejaculating through white lips and chattering teeth," *Who's afraid?* In the wide-spread panic of 1800, the slaveholders appear to have been excessively puzzled to ascertain what could have induced their slaves to engage in such a conspiracy. They, of course, could not have originated such a plot, and had been, in their opinion, so well-treated that *they* could have no motive to wish for their freedom. It was at first rumored that Gabriel had in his possession letters written by white men; then, that the conspiracy of the negroes was "occasioned by the circulation of some artfully written hand-bills, drawn up by the noted Callender in prison, and circulated by two French people of color from Guadaloupe, aided by a United Irish pretended Methodist preacher"; then, "that the instigators of the diabolical plan wished thereby to insure the elections of Adams and Pinckney, and that the blacks, as far as they were capable, reasoned on the Jeffersonian principles of emancipation." They were, at last, unwillingly compelled to believe that the whole plot originated with slaves, and was confined to them exclusively, and that, like all other human beings, deprived by arbitrary power of all their just rights, they were determined to be free.

In a letter written in 1800, by Judge St. George Tucker, of Virginia, and published in Baltimore, he thus speaks:—

"The love of freedom is an inborn sentiment, which the God of nature has planted deep in the heart. Long may it be kept under by the arbitrary institutions of society; but, at the first favorable moment, it springs forth with a power which defies all check. This celestial spark, which fires the breast of the savage, which glows in that of the philosopher, is not extinguished in the bosom of the slave. It may be buried in the embers, but it *still lives,* and the breath of knowledge kindles it into a flame. Thus we find there never have been slaves in any country, who have not seized the first favorable opportunity to revolt. These, our hewers of wood and drawers of water, possess the power of doing us mischief, and are prompted to it by *motives which self-love dictates, which reason justifies.* Our sole security, then, consists in their ignorance of this power, and their means of using it—a security which we have lately found is not to be relied on, and which, small as it is, every day diminishes. Every year adds to the number of those who can read and write; and *the increase of knowledge is the principal agent in evolving the spirit we have to fear.* * * * By way of marking the prodigious change which a few years have made among that class of men, compare the late conspiracy with the revolt under Lord Dunmore. In the one case, a few solitary individuals flocked to that standard, under which they were sure to find protection. In the other, they, in a body, of their own accord, combine a plan for asserting their freedom, and rest their safety on success alone. The difference is, that then they sought freedom merely as a good; now they also claim it as a right. * * * Ignorant and illiterate as they yet are, they have maintained a correspondence, which, whether we consider its extent or duration, is truly astonishing."

Thus far Judge Tucker.

Monday, Sept. 1st, was the day set by General Gabriel and his associates to make the attack on Richmond with fire and sword. The plot was, however, discovered only the day previous, and, as I have been informed, was made known by a slave named Ben, who was unwilling that his master (a Mr. W. who had been very kind to him) should lose his life.

The incidents of this conspiracy were embodied in a song, and set to a tune, both of which were composed by a colored man. The song is still sung.

In the New York *Spectator,* of Sept. 24th, 1800, is a letter dated CHARLESTON, S. C., Sept. 13th, which says that "the negroes have rose in arms against the whites in this country, and have killed several. All the troops of light horse are ordered out by the Governor to suppress the insurrection. Some reports state the number of insurgents, who were

29

embodied about thirty miles from the city, to be about four or five thousand strong. Others decreased this number to seven or eight hundred."

In June, 1816, a conspiracy was formed in Camden, South Carolina; but information of the intent was given by a favorite and confidential slave of Col. Chestnut.

On May 30th, 1822, a "faithful and confidential slave" disclosed to the Intendant of Charleston, S. C., that, on Sunday evening, June 16th, the slaves had determined to rise in rebellion against the whites, "set fire to the Governor's house, seize the Guard-house and Arsenal, and sweep the town with fire and sword, not permitting a white soul to escape." Of the supposed conspirators, one hundred and thirty-one were committed to prison, thirty-five executed, and thirty- seven banished. Of the six ringleaders, Ned Bennet, Peter Poyas, Rolla, Batteau, Jesse, and Denmark Vesey, all were slaves, except Vesey, who had been a slave thirty-eight years, a few man twenty-two years, having in 1800 purchased his freedom.

On July 12th, two slaves were executed; July 26th, twenty-two; July 30th, four; and August 9th, one.

In 1826, the inhabitants of Newbern, Targorough and Hillsborough were alarmed by insurrectionary movements among their slaves. The people of Newbern, being informed that forty slaves were assembled in a swamp, surrounded it, and killed the whole party!!

In August, 1831, there was an insurrection of slaves in Southampton, Virginia, headed by a slave, who called himself Gen. Nat. Turner, who declared to his associates that he was acting under inspired directions, and that the singular appearance of the sun at that time was the signal for them to commence the work of destruction; which resulted in the murder of sixty-four white persons, and more than one hundred slaves were killed. The excitement extended throughout Virginia and the Carolinas. "Another such insurrection," says the Richmond Whig, "will be followed by *putting the whole race to the sword.*" In the same year, insurrections occurred in Martinique, Antigua, St. Jago, Caraccas, and Tortola.

In January, 1832, James McDowell, Jr., in reply to a member who called the Nat. Turner insurrection a "petty affair," thus spoke in the Virginia House of Delegates:—

"Now, sir, I ask you, I ask gentlemen, in conscience to say, was that a 'petty affair' which startled the feelings of your whole population; which threw a portion of it into alarm, a portion of it into panic; which wrung out from an affrigthed people the thrilling cry, day after day, conveyed to your executive, *'We are in peril of our lives—send us an army for defence!'* Was that a 'petty affair,' which drove families from their homes; which assembled women and children in crowds, without shelter, at places of common refuge, in every condition of weakness and infirmity, under every suffering which want and terror could inflict, yet willing to endure all, willing to meet death from famine, death from climate, death from hardships, preferring any thing rather than the horrors of meeting it from a domestic assassin? Was that a 'petty affair,' which erected a peaceful and confiding portion of the State into a military camp; which *outlawed from pity the unfortunate beings whose brothers had offended;* which barred every door, penetrated every bosom with fear or suspicion; which so banished every sense of security from every man's dwelling, that, let but a hoof or horn break upon the silence of the night, and an aching throb would be driven to the heart? The husband would look to his weapon, and the mother would shudder, and weep upon her cradle! Was it the fear of Nat. Turner and his deluded, drunken handful of followers, which produced such effects? Was it this that induced distant counties, where the very name of Southampton was strange, to arm and equip for a struggle? No, sir, it was the *suspicion eternally attached to the slave himself;* the suspicion that a Nat. Turner might be in every family—that the same bloody deed might be acted over at any time, and in any place—that the materials for it were spread through the land, and were always ready for a like explosion. Nothing but the force of this withering apprehension, nothing but the paralyzing and deadening weight with which it falls upon and prostrates the heart of every man who has helpless dependants to protect, nothing but this could have thrown a brave people into consternation, or could have made any portion of this powerful Commonwealth, for a single instant, to have quailed and trembled."

In the same year and month, Henry Berry, Esq., another delegate, thus spoke:—

"Sir, I believe that no cancer on the physical body was ever more certain, steady and fatal in its progress, than this cancer on the political body of

Virginia. It is eating into her very vitals. And shall we admit that the evil is past remedy? Shall we act the part of a puny patient, suffering under the ravages of a fatal disease, who would say the remedy is too painful? Pass as severe laws as you will to keep these unfortunate creatures in ignorance, it is in vain, unless you can extinguish that spark of intellect which God has given them. Sir, we have, as far as possible, closed *every avenue by which light might enter their minds.* We have only to go one step further— to extinguish the capacity to see the light—and our work will be completed. They would then be reduced to the level of the beasts of the field, and we should be safe; and I am not certain that we would not do it, if we could find out the necessary process, and that under the plea of necessity. But, sir, this is impossible; and can man be in the midst of freemen, and not know what freedom is? Can he feel that he has the power to assert his liberty, and *will he not do it?* Yes, sir, *with the certainty of Time's current, he will do it whenever he has the power.* The data are before us all, and every man can work out the process for himself. Sir, a *death-struggle must come between the two classes, [FN#2] in which one or the other will be extinguished forever.* Who can contemplate such a catastrophe as even possible, and be indifferent?"

[FN#2] "Irrepressible Conflict."

In an essay written by Judge St. George Tucker, and published in 1796, he expresses similar sentiments, in language equally forcible, and concludes by saying:—

   "I presume it is possible that an effectual remedy for the evils of slavery may at length be discovered. Whenever that happens, *the golden age of our country will begin.* Till then,
                 ————"Non hospes a hospite tutus
             Non Herus a Famulis, fratrum quoque gratia rara."

"I tremble for my country when I reflect that God is just, that his justice cannot sleep forever," and "that the Almighty has no attribute that can take sides with us in such a contest," viz., "an exchange of situation" [with the slaves,] are the well-known words of Jefferson.

In 1832, a general insurrection of the slaves occurred in Jamaica, when between two and three thousand slaves were killed, and a large number of whites. The loss occasioned by the rebellion was estimated at five millions of dollars, a part of which was occasioned by the burning of one hundred and fifty plantations. *Now,* the British West Indies are forever exempted from all danger of insurrection, while the danger of a servile war in America will, until slavery is abolished, every year increase.

In the month of June, 1839, a vessel, called the Amistad, Ramon Ferrer, Captain, sailed from Havana for Principe, about one hundred leagues distant, with fifty-four negroes and two white passengers, (Spaniards,) viz., Pedro Montez and Jose Ruiz, one of whom claimed to be the owner of the negroes, who were all natives of Africa. While on board, they "suffered much from hunger and thirst." In addition to this, there was much whipping, and "the cook told them that, when they reached land, they would all be eaten." This "made their hearts burn." To avoid being eaten, and to escape the bad treatment, they rose upon the crew with the design of returning to Africa. This was on June 27th, four days after leaving Havana. After killing the captain and the cook, and permitting the crew to escape, they under command of Cinque, who compelled Montez to steer the ship for Africa, which he did in the day time, because the negroes could tell his course by the sun, but put the vessel about in the night. In this manner, the vessel drifted about till August 26th, when she was taken possession of by Capt. Gedney, U. S. N. After an interesting trial in Connecticut, the negroes were set free, and, under the American Missionary Association, were sent to their native country, Africa, and of whom many are now receiving religious instruction by means of missionaries who accompanied them to the Mendi country. It is in relation to these blacks that President Buchanan, in his late message, thus speaks:—"I again recommend that an appropriation be made to be paid to the Spanish Government for the purpose of distribution among the claimants in the Amistad case"!!

On the 27th of October, 1841, the Creole sailed from Richmond with one hundred and thirty-five slaves, bound for New Orleans. On November 7th, they rose on the crew, killed a passenger named Howell, and on November 9th, arrived at Nassau, New Providence, where they were all set free by the British authorities. The leader in this successful attempt to secure their freedom was Madison Washington. "The sagacity, bravery and humanity of this man," says the Hon. William Jay, "do honor to his name, and, but for his complexion, would excite universal admiration."

In 1846, the slaves in Santa Cruz rose in rebellion against their masters, took possession of the island, and thus obtained their freedom, but did no injury to any white person. This was remarkable, as the whites numbered 3,000, and the blacks 25,000.

Now, what is the inference from this list of conspiracies and insurrections, and scores of others which could be collected? Why, (1,) that all danger arises from the continuance of slavery, and not from its abolition. And, (2,) that if the Bible sanctions slavery, the God of the Bible does not. The language of God's providence is one and uniform, and too explicit to be misunderstood. It assures us, and writes the assurance in lines of blood, that the way of the transgressor is hard, and that though hand join in hand, the violators of God's law shall not go unpunished. All history, ancient and modern, is full of examples and warnings on this point. Shall we slight these warnings, shut our eyes against the light, and madly rush on our own destruction? Let us remember that slavery is an unnatural state; that Nature, when her eternal principles are violated, always struggles to restore them to her true estate; and that the natural feelings accord with the sentiment of the poet,

> "If I'm designed yon lordling's slave,
>   By Nature's laws designed,
> Why was an independent wish
>   E'er planted in my mind?"

"If the Bible," says the Rev. Albert Barnes, "could be shown to defend and countenance slavery as a good institution, it would make thousands of infidels; for there are multitudes of minds that will see more clearly that slavery is against all the laws which God has written on the human soul, than they would see that a book, sanctioning such a system, had evidence of divine origin."

Says Charles Alcott, of Medina, Ohio, in his very able lectures on slavery:—"It is easy to show that slavery has, from first to last, been supported directly and solely by crimes, and that the commission of nearly every crime in the Bible calendar, and many crimes against the common law, are absolutely necessary to support it, and give it full effect. It is a fact equally curious and true, that crime of any kind can only be supported by crime; and that, in order to persevere in the commission of one crime, and prevent its detection and punishment, it is necessary to commit still further crimes."

This being true, it follows conclusively that immediate repentance of the sin of slavery is the duty of every master, and immediate emancipation the right of every slave. Says Charles Alcott, "A man cannot stir, or move, or begin to act, either in support of slavery, or in opposition to its immediate abolition, without committing crimes or sins of some sort or other." He cannot be neutral. Therefore, gentle reader, in the *"irrepressible conflict"* that is now agitating the country, and will continue to agitate it till slavery is abolished, which side have you chosen, or do you intend to choose? Will you take the "higher law," which is in harmony with God's providence and his word, or act in favor of the "lower law," which opposes both? If slavery is right, sustain, defend and justify it; but if it is a crime, do all in your power, by moral means, to overthrow the execrable system. If you are a professed Christian, remember the words of Rev. Albert Barnes:—"There is not vital energy enough, there is not power of numbers and influence enough, *out of the Church,* to sustain it. Let every religious denomination in the land detach itself from all connection with slavery. All that is needful is, for each Christian man, for every Christian church, to stand up in the sacred majesty of such a solemn testimony, and to free themselves from all connection with the evil, and utter a calm, deliberate voice to the world, *and the work is done."*

* * *

Published at the Office of the AMERICAN ANTI-SLAVERY SOCIETY, No. 5
Beekman Street, New York. Also, to be had at the Anti-Slavery Offices, No. 21 Cornhill, Boston, and No. 107 North Fifth Street, Philadelphia.